THE EUCHARIST

GOD'S GIFT FOR THE LIFE OF THE WORLD

Foundational theological document
for the 49th International Eucharistic Congress

According to the Statutes of the Pontifical Committee
for the International Eucharistic Congresses

Translated from the French original by Bernadette Gasslein

1073, boul. René-Lévesque Ouest • Québec Canada • G1S 4R5 • (418) 687-6086

Scripture quotations are taken from the *New Revised Standard Version* of the Bible (*NRSV*).

Quotations from papal, conciliar and synodal documents are taken from the English translations found on the Vatican website, www.vatican.va.

Legal deposit: Bibliothèque et Archives nationales du Québec, 2006
Library and Archives Canada, 2006
All rights reserved © Diocèse de Québec, 2006
ISBN-10 2-89129-523-4
ISBN-13 978-2-89129-523-9
Printed in Canada

www.annesigier.qc.ca

TABLE OF CONTENTS

INVITATION 7

INTRODUCTION – **Do this in Memory of Me: Remembering God Today** 11

PART ONE – **The Holy Eucharist, God's Gift** 17

I. The Eucharist, God's Gift par excellence 17

   A. At the Centre and Summit of Salvation History . 17

   B. The Institution of the Holy Eucharist 21

II. The Eucharist, Memorial of the Paschal Mystery .. 24

   A. Memorial of Christ's Passover, a Trinitarian Gift 24

   B. The Paschal Sacrifice 27

PART TWO – **The Eucharist, the New Covenant** 31

III. The Eucharist Builds up the Church, the Sacrament of Salvation 31

   A. The Gift of the Church as Communion 32

      1) Mary, First Church and Eucharistic Woman . 32

      2) People of God and Sacrament of Salvation .. 34

      3) Bride of the Lamb and Body of Christ 35

   B. The Church's Eucharistic Response 38

      1) To Believe and Love Like Mary, in Jesus 38

      2) To Be Reconciled in Unity 40

      3) To Come Together on Sunday, the Lord's Day 42

PART THREE – **For the Life of the World** 45
IV. The Eucharist, the Life of Christ in our Lives 45
    A. The Spiritual Worship of the Baptized 45
    B. Authentic Adoration 48
    C. The Ministers of the New Covenant 52

V. Eucharist and Mission 54
    A. Evangelization and the Transformation
       of the World 55
    B. Constructing Peace through Justice and Charity . 58

VI. Witnesses to Eucharist in the Midst of the World . 61
    A. The Universal call to Holiness 61
    B. The Family, the Domestic Church,
       Foundation of a Civilization of Love 62
    C. Consecrated life, Pledge of hope
       that Proclaims the Bridegroom's Coming 64

CONCLUSION – **God so loved the World** 67

INVITATION

The Eucharist, Christ's presence and gift to the world, will be at the heart of a huge gathering of Christians from all continents in Quebec City, June 15-22, 2008, for the 49th International Eucharistic Congress.

As the Archbishop of Quebec and Primate of Canada, I am happy to welcome all those who will join us for this great celebration of the Church assembled in prayer, sharing and communion.

Pope John Paul II chose Quebec City as the land of welcome for this Eucharistic congress.

Quebec City enjoys a unique heritage among North American cities because of its leading role in the exploration of the continent and the first proclamation of the Gospel to its aboriginal people. Today, Quebec City has a population of close to half a million people. Each year, it welcomes thousands of visitors who are drawn by its spectacular setting and unique architecture, which has been designated as a World Heritage Site and is now protected by the United Nations Educational, Scientific and Cultural Organization (UNESCO). The year 2008 will mark the 400th anniversary of its foundation.

INVITATION

At the beginning of the third millennium of Christianity, the Catholic Church, conscious of the phenomenon of globalization, is concerned about everything that can promote a civilization of love and peace. The Church draws from the Holy Eucharist the inspiration and energy that spur on the involvement of all in building a more just and fraternal world. Thus, the theme chosen for this congress: The Eucharist, God's gift for the life of the world. This theme is developed in the foundational theological document that I am honoured to present to the public after it has been approved by the Pontifical Council for International Eucharistic Congresses.

This document develops some aspects of Eucharistic doctrine, in particular, that of the memorial of Christ's Paschal Mystery. It is important to give new life to the memory of the Christian origins of this continent so that we can bring to life and transmit the gospel values and the importance of the Eucharist in today's world. Nor can we forget the washing of feet and the saying that can change the world: Love one another as I have loved you (see *Jn* 15.12).

I would like to thank the team of theologians, scripture scholars and catechists, directed by His Excellency, Bishop Pierre-André Fournier, and assisted by Msgr. Jean Picher, the general secretary of the Congress, and Sister Doris Lamontagne, p.f.m., assistant general secretary, who collaborated generously on this text. The homilies and catechesis inspired by this text will help the delegates to prepare spiritually and will nourish the prayer of many people who will join the celebration of this congress in spirit.

The Archdiocese of Quebec warmly welcomes the visitors and faithful who will participate in this event in an ecumenical spirit. Conscious of its weaknesses, but strong in God's faithfulness, the Church in Quebec is proud to present to the universal Church a history of holiness that Pope John Paul recognized during his pontificate, when he beatified or canonized 14 well-known personages from Quebec.

May the celebration of this International Congress, in deep communion with His Holiness, Benedict XVI, bring to each member of the Church renewed hope and a livelier awareness of God's gift for the life of the world.

Marc Cardinal Ouellet
Archbishop of Quebec
Primate of Canada

INTRODUCTION

Do this in Memory of Me: Remembering God Today

The International Eucharistic Congress that will be held in Quebec City in June 2008 offers both the local Church and the universal Church an intense time to pray, reflect on, and celebrate the gift of the Holy Eucharist. The forty-ninth in a series of congresses that have marked the Church's life for more than a century, the Quebec conference coincides with the 400th anniversary of the foundation of the first French city in North America, which would become in the 17th century an important entry point for missionary activity on the entire continent.

The Eucharistic congress will be a *statio orbis*, which means that, at the invitation of the local Church in Quebec, the universal Church will celebrate and remember God's gift offered to all humanity, the Eucharist. The city of Quebec, with its motto, "God's gift I will treasure" stands at the heart of the history of a people whose motto proclaims "I remember." This motto reminds us of the mandate that Jesus gave to his apostles at the Last Supper: Do this in memory of me (*Lk* 22.19).

As the biblical sense of this term indicates, the Eucharist – the memorial of the Passover of the Lord – not only remembers, but makes present the salvific event. The Eucharistic Congress will be a privileged event during which we pay homage to this gift of God at the heart of the Christian life and recall the Christian roots of many countries that await a new evangelization. The Eucharist nourished the proclamation of the Gospel and the encounter between the European and indigenous civilizations on this continent. Today it still acts as a leaven in our culture and continues to hold out a measure of hope for the future of a world on the path of globalization.

The world's longing for the freedom of love

The central theme of the Congress, approved by Pope Benedict XVI, is "The Eucharist, God's gift for the life of the world." It is particularly important today to remember God's gift, for, in the midst of remarkable technological progress, notably in the area of communication, our world experiences a deep interior emptiness that it perceives as an absence of God. Fascinated by its own creative capacities, contemporary humanity tends to forget its

Creator and set itself up as the sole master of its own destiny.

This temptation to put ourselves in God's place does not silence the longing for the infinite that inhabits our depths and the authentic values that we strive to develop, even if they do risk leading us astray. The value we place on freedom, our longing for equality, the ideal of solidarity, our access to unrestricted communications, our technological abilities and the protection of the environment are unquestionably admirable values that are a credit to our world and bring forth fruits of justice and brotherhood.

The tragedy of a humanism that has forgotten God

In addition, forgetting the Creator risks closing human beings in on themselves, in a self-centredness that results in an inability to love and make lasting commitments, and increasingly frustrates the universal longing for love and freedom. For man, created in God's image and for communion with God, "cannot fully find himself except through a sincere gift of himself." [1] The fulfillment of the human person

---

1. Second Vatican Council, Pastoral Constitution on the Church in the Modern World, *Gaudium et Spes,* n. 24.

comes about by this self-gift that signifies openness to the other, welcome and respect for life.

But today human beings are constantly pushing back the limits of our mastery over the transmission and end of life. Unchecked, this power over life and death, although technologically possible, threatens humanity itself. For, in the strong words of Pope John Paul II, a "culture of death" has taken over many secularized societies. The death of God in the culture leads almost inevitably to the death of the human being. We see this, not only in currents of nihilistic thought, but above all in the conflictual and broken relationships that are multiplying at all levels of human experience, disrupting marriage and the family, multiplying ethnic and social conflicts, and increasing the gulf between the rich and the huge majority who are the poor.

Despite our keener consciousness of human dignity and human rights, we are witnessing the multiplication of violations of these rights almost everywhere on the planet: the accumulation of weapons of mass destruction, which make a lie of all talk of peace; a growing concentration of material goods in the hands of a few, which skews the spread of globalization, while, to our shame, the fundamental needs of masses of the poor are ignored. World peace is undermined by injustice and misery, and terrorism becomes the weapon of choice of the desperate.

On the religious level, people today are no longer willing to submit themselves to an authority that dictates their conduct. They must cope with widespread access to many different beliefs and the growing difficulty of handing on to new generations the heritage that they have received from their own religious tradition. The Christian faith is no exception to this pattern, and is even more affected by it because its transmission relies on revelation that reason alone cannot measure. Jealous of their hard-won freedom, human beings construct their own spirituality without any reference to religion, thus sometimes giving in to the excessively individualistic tendencies of contemporary democratic cultures.

The holy Eucharist contains the essential elements of a Christian response to the drama of a humanism that has lost its constitutive point of reference to the God who is creator and redeemer.

The Eucharist remembers God's saving action. As the memorial of the death and resurrection of Jesus Christ, it brings to the world the gospel of Christ's definitive peace, for which we always hope in the present life. In celebrating the holy Eucharist in the name of all humanity redeemed by Jesus Christ, the Church welcomes the gift that God promised us: "But the Advocate, the Holy Spirit, whom the Father will send in my name, will teach you everything, and remind you of all that I have said to you" (*Jn* 14.26). God definitively remembers the divine covenant with humanity and gives the divine self as food for eternal life: "He remembers his love" sings the Virgin Mary in her *Magnificat* (*Lk* 1.54).

PART ONE

The Holy Eucharist, God's Gift

I - The Eucharist, God's Gift par excellence

A new covenant

A. At the Centre and Summit of Salvation History

"The Church has received the Eucharist from Christ her Lord not as one gift – however precious – among so many others, but as the gift par excellence, for it is the gift of himself, of his person in his sacred humanity, as well as the gift of his saving work". [2]

The servant of God, John Paul II, ended and crowned his long pontificate during the year of the Eucharist that he set up following his encyclical *Ecclesia de Eucharistia*. He wanted to rekindle in the heart of the Church an admiration for this supreme gift of the Holy Eucharist and stir up renewed adoration of this Sacrament which contains the very Person of the Lord Jesus in his sacred humanity. The

---

2. John Paul II, Encyclical Letter, *Ecclesia de Eucharistia*, n. 11.

October 2005 Synod of Bishops on *The Eucharist in the Life and Mission of the Church* prolonged and deepened this reflection by spelling out the pastoral implications of the Eucharistic mystery.

God had prepared for this gift of gifts throughout the whole course of salvation history. The Holy Eucharist is the recapitulation and crown of God's many gifts to humanity since the creation of the world. It fulfils God's plan to establish a definitive covenant with humanity. Despite the tragic story of sin and rejection that has marked history since its origins, God clearly institutes by this sacrament the New Covenant sealed in the Blood of Christ. This covenant definitively seals a long history of covenant between God and the children of Abraham, our father in faith. Like the celebration of the Jewish Passover in the era of the Promise, the Holy Eucharist accompanies the pilgrimage of God's people throughout the time of the New Covenant. The Eucharist is a living memorial of the gift that Jesus Christ made of his own Body and Blood to redeem humanity from sin and death, and give us eternal life.

Over the thousands of years of its liturgy and prayers, the Jewish people learned to celebrate the greatness of its most holy God who is creator and liberator. Passover always stood at the centre of its liturgy, remembering from age to age the event of the Exodus: "This day shall be a day of remembrance for you" (*Ex* 12.14).

Celebrated by generations of believers, Passover is rooted in the foundational event of the first Covenant: God's intervention to deliver the Hebrew people from Egypt and lead them through the Red Sea. "Israel saw the great work that the Lord did against the Egyptians. So the people feared the Lord and believed in the Lord and in his servant Moses" (*Ex* 14.31). This foundational event would be sealed on Sinai by the sacred gift of the Law and the people's commitment: "See the blood of the covenant that the Lord has made with you in accordance with all these words" (*Ex* 24.8). And the people replied, "All that the Lord has spoken we will do" (*Ex* 24.7).

This first "passage" of one segment of humanity from slavery to freedom announced and prepared the decisive intervention of the living God and Father in favour of humankind, the sending of his last Word, a personal and definitive Word, in the incarnation of the Word. Thus, at a particular moment in human history "the grace of God has appeared, bringing salvation to all," (*Titus* 2.11). The Church's grateful memory proclaims it: "Father, you so loved the world that in the fullness of time you sent your only Son to be our Saviour."[3]

The coming of the Word made flesh marks the crowning point of the gift of the divine self: "Long ago God spoke to our ancestors in many and various ways by the prophets, but in these last days he has spoken to us by a Son, whom he appointed heir of all things, through whom he also created the worlds" (*Heb* 1.1-2). The Letter to the Hebrews teaches that the New Covenant worship in Christ's Blood is based on and established by the incarnation of God's Son and the sacrificial offering of his life. This worship, begun by Jesus Christ, fulfils the beginnings of worship found in the first Covenant by offering a single sacrifice, once and for all, unlike the animal sacrifices of the ancient Law, because it is the sacrifice of the spotless Lamb, "who through the eternal Spirit offered himself without blemish to God" so we might "worship the living God!" (*Heb* 9.14). Through the Holy Eucharist – the summit of God's gift, the Word made flesh and life-giving Spirit at the source of the worship of the New Covenant –, Christ makes this eternal worship present here and now.

---

3. *Roman Missal,* Preface, Eucharistic Prayer IV.

B. The Institution of the Holy Eucharist

An event forever new

"At the Last Supper, on the night when He was betrayed, our Saviour instituted the Eucharistic sacrifice of His Body and Blood. He did this in order to perpetuate the sacrifice of the Cross throughout the centuries until He should come again, and so to entrust to His beloved spouse, the Church, a memorial of His death and resurrection: a sacrament of love, a sign of unity, a bond of charity, a paschal banquet in which Christ is eaten, the mind is filled with grace, and a pledge of future glory is given to us."[4]

What the Saviour instituted on the night he was betrayed was the gift of himself, impelled by the depths of his love: "Now before the festival of the Passover, Jesus knew that his hour had come to depart from this world and go to the Father. Having loved his own who were in the world, he loved them to the end" (*Jn* 13.1). The institution of the Holy Eucharist is the gift of Love in Person; it is God who gives himself in the Sacrament of the Passover of Christ. Jesus instituted this Sacrament by a rite that continues the gift of his life as a sacrifice that takes away sin, and he conveyed its meaning by a gesture of service, the washing of feet.

---

4. Second Vatican Council, Constitution on the Sacred Liturgy, *Sacrosanctum Concilium*, n. 47.

The memorial meal of the Jewish Passover enabled the people of Israel to remember their covenant with God and, by its rites, to relive God's real and efficacious intervention in their history. The evening of Holy Thursday, Jesus knew that he was bringing to its fulfillment the memorial of the Jewish Passover meal: he took bread, blessed it and said, "Take this, all of you, and eat it. This is my body which will be given up for you."; then he took the cup filled with wine and said, "Take this, all of you, and drink from it; this is the cup of my blood, the blood of the new and everlasting covenant. It will be shed for you and for all. *Do this in memory of me.*" By these gestures and words, Jesus instituted a new rite, his paschal rite, by which he offered himself in place of the traditional lamb, giving himself and sacrificing himself out of love. His act of love fulfills the New Covenant in his Blood, which frees humanity from sin and death.

Always impelled by the same love, the risen Christ, in the power of the Holy Spirit, makes the gift of his Eucharist present each time his Church celebrates the rite received from Him at the Last Supper, on the night before his Passion. In celebrating this sacramental rite, the Church is intimately associated with the offering of Jesus Christ and thus with the exercise of his priestly function for the worship of

God and the salvation of humanity. "Christ indeed always associates the Church with Himself in this great work wherein God is perfectly glorified and men are sanctified. The Church is his beloved Bride who calls to her Lord, and through Him offers worship to the Eternal Father."[5]

The institution of the Eucharist conceals a profound mystery that transcends our ability to understand and our categories. It is the mystery of faith par excellence. The Eucharist constantly nourishes the Church, for from the Eucharist the Church draws her life and her reason for existence. At the Last Supper, Jesus gave the gift of his sacramental presence, a "real and substantial presence"[6], even though it is veiled in the humble signs of bread and wine. He enjoined the Church to welcome in perpetuity his declaration of love and the gift of his Body and his Blood as an event, always new and renewed, that constantly wells up from his Eucharistic heart. Here we find the deep meaning of "memorial", which, already in the Jewish tradition, has the sense of an objective event, not only a subjective act of remembering the past. Celebrating this memorial plunges the participants once more into the mystery of the Passover of the Lord.

---

5. *Ibid.*, n. 7.

6. Council of Trent, *Decretum de SS Eucharistia*, Chapter 1.

II - The Eucharist, Memorial of the Paschal Mystery

A. Memorial of Christ's Passover, a Trinitarian Gift

Presence of the risen Christ

What, then, is the content of this memorial that the Church, since its origins, has celebrated as the Lord's gift par excellence? Jesus established its essential form at the Last Supper when he spoke the words of institution over the bread and the wine to change them into his Body and Blood. But this act by which Christ gives his own person conceals a content whose depths cannot be exhausted since it contains the whole Passover of the Lord, that is, his offering to the Father of love unto death on the Cross and his Resurrection from the dead by the power of the Holy Spirit.

When the Church celebrates the Eucharist, it welcomes the gift of Christ who hands himself over to sinners out of obedience to the Father's will. St. Paul proclaims it solemnly in the hymn to the Philippians: "he humbled himself and became obedient to the point of death – even death on a cross. Therefore God also highly exalted Him and gave Him the name that is above every name, so that at the name of Jesus every knee should bend, in heaven and on earth and under the earth, and every tongue should confess that Jesus Christ is Lord, to the glory of God the Father (*Phil* 2.8-11).

Thus the Church welcomes the Father's gift to the world in his only Son, incarnate and crucified: "For God so loved the world that he gave his only Son, so that everyone who believes in Him may not perish but may have eternal life" (*Jn* 3.16). "See with what magnificent generosity God outdoes human beings," writes Origen. "Abraham offered to God his mortal son who did not die, and God gave up his immortal Son who died for all of us."[7] The sacrifice of Isaac in the Old Covenant announced and prepared the consummate sacrifice of the New Covenant, that of the true Lamb.

The act of love of the Son who gives himself up corresponds perfectly to the act of love of the Father who gives Him up, and this perfect correspondence of the love of Father and Son for us is confirmed by the Holy Spirit who raises Christ from the dead. In the same way the Spirit confirms the divine authority of Jesus' preaching and deeds, justifying at the same time the total assent required by Christian faith. Here is the heart of the Good News that the Church

---

7. Origen, *Homily on Genesis* (8, 8: PG 12, 208), in *The Liturgy of the Hours,* Vol. III (New York: Catholic Book Publishing Corp., 1975), p. 180. See *Gen* 22.10.

from the beginning has announced to all nations and that it celebrates in each Eucharist: "The gospel concerning his Son, who was descended from David according to the flesh and was declared to be Son of God with power according to the spirit of holiness by resurrection from the dead, Jesus Christ our Lord" (*Rom* 1.3-4). The supreme gift of the Eucharist makes present the risen Christ and his whole life and paschal mystery.

This Trinitarian gift reconciles the world with God by the love-offering unto death of the Son and by his resurrection which confirms the victory of Trinitarian love over sin and death.

By his own gift – a gift that in glorifying the Son also glorifies the Father who sent the Son – the Holy Spirit confirms the perfect communion of the Father and the Son at the heart of the Paschal Mystery. This is why the communion of the faithful in the Body and Blood of Christ is also a communion with the Holy Spirit. "Saint Ephrem writes: 'He called the bread his living body and he filled it with himself and his Spirit… He who eats it with faith, eats Fire and Spirit… Take and eat this, all of you, and eat with it the Holy Spirit. For it is truly my body and whoever eats it will have eternal life.'" [8]

---

8. John Paul II, Encyclical Letter, *Ecclesia de Eucharistia*, n. 17.

B. The Paschal Sacrifice

Effective sign of God's gift

Because the Eucharist is the memorial of Christ's Passover, it is also a sacrifice – so the *Catechism of the Catholic Church* insistently reminds us.[9] "For them, I give myself" Jesus confides to his disciples in his final prayer (*Jn* 17.18). When his hour has come, Jesus does not shy away from his Father's will; he loves the Father and surrenders himself freely into the hands of human beings out of love for his Father and for sinners. The Eucharist is the memorial of this sacrifice, that is, of this act of redemptive love that reestablishes the communion of humanity with God by overcoming the obstacle posed by the world's sin.

Throughout history, humanity's disobedience has constantly broken the covenant relationship with God. Christ's loving obedience redeems all the sinful disobedience of the sons and daughters of Adam. "A sacrifice that the Father accepted, giving, in return for this total self-giving by his Son, who 'became obedient unto death' (*Phil* 2.8), his own paternal gift, that is to say the grant of new immortal life in the resurrection."[10]. This exchange reestablishes the communication and communion between heaven and earth,

---

9. See the *Catechism of the Catholic Church*, n. 1365.
10. John Paul II, Encyclical Letter, *Ecclesia de Eucharistia*, n. 13. See also *Redemptor hominis*, n. 20.

between the God who is love and humanity who is called to communion with God's love by faith. Christ's sacrifice is thus a Paschal Sacrifice, a total gift of self by which all humanity "passes over" from the slavery of sin to the liberty of the children of God. "Very truly, I tell you,… those who eat my flesh and drink my blood have eternal life, and I will raise them up on the last day" (Jn 6.53,54).

For God's Son, this real sacrifice entails an unmeasurable measure of suffering, including his descent into the abyss of death. The Gospels recount some aspects of Jesus' passion that reveal the depth of his suffering and his love.

The Lord's thirst on the cross, his wounds, his sense of being abandoned, his loud cry and his pierced heart allow us to imagine to some extent all his suffering – bodily, moral and spiritual. "His death on the Cross is the culmination of that turning of God against himself in which he gives himself in order to raise man up and save him. This is love in its most radical form."[11]

As we contemplate this love that suffers and dies on the Cross, we learn the measure of the measureless love of Christ's heart and discover the immensity of the gift of the Holy Sacrament of the Eucharist.

---

11. Benedict XVI, Encyclical Letter, *Deus Caritas est*, n. 12.

In light of this doctrine, we understand even better why all the sacramental life of the Church and of each Christian reaches its summit and its fullness in the Eucharist. In this Sacrament, the mystery of Christ's sacrificial self-offering to the Father on the altar of the Cross is renewed continuously by his own will. And the Father responds to his offering by the new life of the Risen One. This new life, shown forth in the glorified Body of the risen Christ, has become the effective sign of the new gift to humanity. "But the point is that Christ's Resurrection is something more, something different. If we may borrow the language of the theory of evolution, it is the greatest 'mutation,' absolutely the most crucial leap into a totally new dimension that there has ever been in the long history of life and its development: a leap into a completely new order which does concern us, and concerns the whole of history." [12]

The Eucharist, as the memorial of the death and resurrection of the Lord, thus does much more than recall a past event: it represents sacramentally an event that is always "now" – since Jesus' offering of love on the cross was accepted by the Father and glorified by the Holy Spirit. Consequently this offering transcends time and space, and by the Lord's explicit

---

12. Benedict XVI, Homily, Easter Vigil, April 15, 2006.

will, remains permanently available to the faith of the Church. "Do this in memory of me." When the Church celebrates the Eucharistic banquet, she does not do "as if" it were the first time. Rather, the Church welcomes the definitive eschatological event, the event of a unique love that is always offered to us. This banquet of love takes its inexhaustible substance from the sacrifice of love of the Son of God made man, who has been lifted up and always intercedes for us.

PART TWO

The Eucharist, the New Covenant

III - The Eucharist Builds up the Church, the Sacrament of Salvation

The supreme gift of the Eucharist is a covenant mystery, the nuptial mystery joining God and humanity. In the Eucharist the living God constantly gives rebirth to the Church as a people brought together, as the Body and Spouse of Christ, as a living community that is at the same time a single mystical Person with Him. Saint Augustine says, "Let us rejoice then and give thanks that we have become not only Christians, but Christ himself." [13]

The Church is the people of the New Covenant, as inseparable from the Eucharist as the body is inseparable from the head, living from the Eucharist as a wife lives from the gift of her husband. As heir to and partner in the Eucharistic mystery, the Church,

---

13. Saint Augustine, *In ev. Jo.* (21, 8: PL 35, 1568). See the *Catechism of the Catholic Church*, n. 795.

quickened by the Spirit and shaped by Mary's faith, participates in God's gift to the world. The Church herself is a sacrament, that is, "a sign and instrument both of a very closely knit union with God and of the unity of the whole human race."[14] Indeed, the Church is the universal sacrament of Trinitarian communion for the world.

A. The Gift of the Church as Communion

1) Mary, First Church and Eucharistic Woman

Mary, Eucharistic woman

God's gift to the world came about thanks to a woman, blessed among all women, who believed and handed herself over unconditionally to the mysterious Word of her Lord. Mary of Nazareth is the woman who, above all others, said "yes" to the God of the covenant, thus becoming at the annunciation, the fulfilment of the daughter of Sion, the beginning of the Church. Her "yes" accompanied the incarnation of God's Word from the first moment of his conception to his death and Resurrection. No other creature possesses such a concrete memory of the Word enfleshed even unto Eucharistic flesh.

---

14. Second Vatican Council, Dogmatic Constitution on the Church, *Lumen Gentium*, n. 1.

No other human being knows so perfectly what the mercy, pardon, compassion and suffering of redeeming Love means.

Nothing suggests that Mary was present at the Last Supper, when the rite of the New Covenant was established, but she stood at the foot of the Cross, where the Holy Sacrifice of the Lamb who takes away the sin of the world was consummated.

Mary is the Eucharistic woman par excellence [15], the new Eve whose utter openness allows the fecundity of the new Adam to take its course. "Mater Dei et Mater Ecclesiae" (*She is Mother of God and Mother of the Church*). In her and by her, the Church already communes perfectly with the Cross, with the sacrificial offering of the Son of God. Destined, like Mary, to the glory of being the spouse of the Lamb, the Church contemplates Mary at the foot of the Cross as the glorious and sorrowful icon of its own mystery of communion. With the spotless Virgin who then becomes the fertile mother of the whole reconciled human race, the Church, by the pure grace of the God who is love, learns to be in communion with the redeeming and nuptial love of the sacrificial Lamb.

---

15. See John Paul II, Encyclical Letter, *Ecclesia de Eucharistia*, nn. 53-58.

2) People of God and Sacrament of Salvation

The Church, sacrament of salvation

Within the framework of the Eucharistic meal the Church welcomes and accomplishes in the most special manner its profound mystery of communion. Jesus' gift which it commemorates, in fidelity to his Word, is the basis of and nourishment for the Covenant relationship between Jesus and the Church, on behalf of all humanity. Jesus' Paschal Banquet draws the Church into his Trinitarian love that comes from the Father, the first source, and from the ultimate gift, the Holy Spirit.

Indeed it is the Father who calls humanity to the wedding feast of his Son (*Mt* 22.1-14), the Paschal Banquet where he himself serves the Lamb sacrificed since the foundation of the world as well as the cup of the Kingdom which communicates the inebriation of the Spirit of which St. Peter speaks on the day of Pentecost. Thus, by giving to the Church his Son and his Spirit, the Father associates the Church to his mystery of love and fruitfulness. He raises her up and ennobles her by welcoming her to his own heavenly table where love is the only food and the eternal source of life.

As the people of God assembled in unity, the Church, mystery of Trinitarian communion meant for all humanity, is the sacrament of salvation. God calls this people together; to serve the New Covenant the Spirit organizes this people according to different hierarchical functions and many charismatic ministries. The Church expresses her full ecclesial vitality and assures her unity by the sacramental communion of her members in Christ's Body and Blood. "Grant that we, who are nourished by his body and blood, may be filled with his Holy Spirit, and become one body, one spirit in Christ." [16]

At each Mass, the prayer of the epiclesis takes up the prayer of Jesus himself for the unity of his disciples: "The glory that you have given me I have given them, so that they may be one, as we are one" (*Jn* 17.22). The Holy Spirit, invoked on the offerings and the assembly, is the glory of Trinitarian communion at work in each Eucharistic Celebration.

This is why the Church, the people of God and sacrament of salvation, must let herself be called together and assembled, open herself to the understanding of the scriptures, be constantly reconciled and enter into communion with eternal Life here below by the Easter sacrament.

3) *Bride of the Lamb and Body of Christ*

A wedding feast

God counts on the Church, his humble partner, to be able to give the divine self to the world in this

---

16. *Roman Missal*, Eucharistic Prayer III.

mystery of Covenant. Although poor and fragile because of the sinfulness of her children, the Church commits herself by plunging over and over again into the grace of her baptism through penance and the holy Eucharist. The more the Church is conscious of sheltering the mystery of the thrice-holy God, and of being called to respond to God, not just in an exemplary fashion, but even in a nuptial manner, the more she should try to purify and reform herself. For "[t]he entire Christian life bears the mark of the spousal love of Christ and the Church. Already Baptism, the entry into the People of God, is a nuptial mystery; it is, so to speak the nuptial bath which precedes the wedding feast, the Eucharist."[17]

At the climax of the Eucharistic prayer, the Church puts this acclamation in the mouth of its minister: "The mystery of faith!" This jubilant shout recognizes what is happening, that is, the transformation of the bread and wine into the Body and Blood of Christ by the power of the Holy Spirit. It also recognizes the mystery of the New Covenant, the nuptial encounter of Christ, the Spouse, who gives himself, and of the Church as Bride who welcomes Him and unites herself to his offering. By the power of the Word and the epiclesis of the Spirit on the

---

17. *Catechism of the Catholic Church*, n. 1617.

Eucharistic species, the living Christ, whose death we proclaim until he comes again, unites to himself the Church community as his body and his spouse. He transforms the offering of the assembled community into his own body and gives to the Church in communion his Eucharistic body as a wedding present.

"This is a great mystery" exclaims the apostle Paul in reference to the union of Christ and the Church as the model and the mystery of sacramental marriage (*Eph* 5.32). Saint Ambrose sees in the Eucharist Christ's wedding present to his Spouse and, in communion, Love's kiss. And Cabasilas can rightly observe, "'This is a great mystery,' said blessed Paul (*Eph* 5.22), referring to this union. This is the celebrated marriage by which the most holy Bridegroom espouses the Church as His Bride. It is here that Christ feeds the choir that surrounds Him; by this Mystery alone we become 'flesh of his flesh, and bone of his bones'" (*Gen* 2.21).[18]

"The Eucharist draws us into Jesus' act of self-oblation. More than just statically receiving the incarnate Logos, we enter into the very dynamic of his self-giving. The imagery of marriage between

---

18. Nicholas Cabasilas, *The Life in Christ,* translated from the Greek by Carmino J. de Catanzara (New York: St. Vladimir's Seminary Press, 1974, Book IV, § 7, p. 123.

God and Israel is now realized in a way previously inconceivable: it had meant standing in God's presence, but now it becomes union with God through sharing in Jesus' self-gift, sharing in his Body and Blood. The sacramental 'mysticism', grounded in God's condescension towards us, operates at a radically different level and lifts us to far greater heights than anything that any human mystical elevation could ever accomplish."[19]

B. The Church's Eucharistic Response

1) *To Believe and Love Like Mary, in Jesus*

As I have loved you

God's gift to the banquet of love commits the Church to sharing this gift with the whole of humanity, which is called to become Christ's body and spouse. The Church's primary devotion to this mystery is its full, marvelling, worshipping faith. For, in response to the ultimate mystery of God's Eucharistic self-offering, must correspond the supreme mystery of faith: the Church's total, gratitude-filled adherence, united with Mary's pure faith. The Holy Spirit's mission is to assure this nuptial relationship between the perpetual realization of the Eucharistic mystery and the Church's welcome that thus nourishes the world's hope by its witness.

---

19. Benedict XVI, Encyclical Letter, *Deus caritas est*, n. 13.

The first form of sharing that springs immediately from the Eucharistic heart of Jesus is the new commandment of love: "I give you a new commandment, that you love one another. Just as I have loved you, you also should love one another" (*Jn* 13.34). This commandment is new because its measure is no longer to love the neighbour as ourselves, but as Jesus loved. It is new because it puts before us the essential demand of entering into the eschatological community of disciples who are united to Him by the same faith; it is new in the measure that it requires humility and a willingness to serve that enables us to take the last place and die for others.

"Dear brethren, the Lord has marked out for us the fullness of love that we ought to have for each other. He tells us: 'No one has greater love than the man who lays down his life for his friends' ... John the evangelist, who recorded [these words], draws the conclusion in one of his letters: 'As Christ laid down his life for us, so we too ought to lay down our lives for our brothers.' We should indeed love one another as he loved us, he who laid down his life for us."[20]

"Union with Christ is also union with all those to whom he gives himself. I cannot possess Christ just

---

20. Saint Augustine, *Homily on the Gospel of John* (Tract. 84, 1-2: CCL 36, 536-638), in *The Liturgy of the Hours,* Vol. II (New York: Catholic Book Publishing Corp., 1976), p. 449.

for myself; I can belong to Him only in union with all those who have become, or who will become, his own. Communion draws me out of myself towards Him, and thus also towards unity with all Christians.

"We become 'one body,' completely joined in a single existence. Love of God and love of neighbour are now truly united: God incarnate draws us all to himself. We can thus understand how *agape* also became a term for the Eucharist: there God's own *agape* comes to us bodily, in order to continue his work in us and through us. Only by keeping in mind this Christological and sacramental basis can we correctly understand Jesus' teaching on love."[21]

Reconciled in unity

2) To Be Reconciled in Unity

The Eucharistic Celebration makes Christ's disciples aware of their responsibility for their own ongoing need to be reconciled and to be artisans of reconciliation. They express this by celebrating the Sacrament of Reconciliation that purifies their hearts for Eucharistic Communion and by their decisions to welcome each other with their different cultures and life choices. They also express it when they ask for forgiveness, when they offer intercessory prayer for all, when they pray the Lord's Prayer, exchange the

---

21. Benedict XVI, Encyclical Letter, *Deus Caritas est*, n. 14.

sign of peace, share one bread and one cup, want to take Communion to the sick or stand in solidarity with the poor and the marginalized. Such are many of the signs of this love for brothers and sisters that each assembly tries to live and which constantly builds up the Body of Christ: "By this everyone will know that you are my disciples, if you have love for one another" (*Jn* 13.35).

"Christ the Lord founded one Church and one Church only. However, many Christian communions present themselves to men as the true inheritors of Jesus Christ ... Such division openly contradicts the will of Christ, scandalizes the world, and damages the holy cause of preaching the Gospel to every creature."[22]

That around the world the Christian Churches celebrate the Lord's Supper separately is a sign of historical and doctrinal differences that it is impossible to conceal or overlook. United by one and the same baptism, Christ's disciples cannot forget the consequences of their divisions on their individual or collective witness to the world. The realization that they cannot all gather in full communion at the same table and sorrow over the resulting weakening

---

22. Second Vatican Council, Decree on Ecumenism, *Unitatis Redintegratio*, n. 1.

of the missionary witnessing opens hearts to a search for reconciliation among all the members of the Body of Christ, "so that they may be one" (Jn 17.11). Each Eucharist is celebrated in anticipation of, and hope for the reunification of the one people of God at the one table of the Lord.

3) To Come Together on Sunday, the Lord's Day

Sunday, a sacrament of Easter

The Church is the community of disciples that professes its belonging to the Lord by its distinctive sign: the practise of mutual love and fraternal love for all. We cannot love with the same love as Christ without constantly receiving this love from Him. His new commandment is not a simple moral ideal offered for our freedom. It is a covenant, a love shared between the Lord and his disciples, which increases and shines on the world if it is constantly renewed at its source, the Sunday Eucharist.

The Lord appeared for the first time on Easter Sunday evening in the upper room, and then returned eight days later to encounter Thomas the Doubter. These appearances confirmed the disciples' faith and prepared them for the Lord's presence in a new form: in the Sacraments and, in a special way, in the Sunday Eucharist. "'We celebrate Sunday because of the venerable Resurrection of our Lord Jesus Christ, and we do so not only at Easter but also at each turning of the week': so wrote Pope Innocent I at the beginning of the fifth century, testifying to an already well-established practise which had evolved from the early years after the Lord's Resurrection. Saint Basil speaks of 'holy Sunday, honoured by the Lord's Resurrection, the first fruits of all the other days'; and Saint Augustine calls Sunday 'a sacrament of Easter.'"[23]

Indeed, Sunday is the day when, more than any other day, Christians are called to remember the salvation offered to them in their baptism, and which made them a new creation in Christ: "When you were buried with Him in baptism, you were also raised with Him through faith in the power of God, who raised Him from the dead" (*Col* 2.12; see also *Rom* 6.4-6). When Christians come together for the Sunday assembly, they are not primarily obeying a precept. Their presence witnesses to their identity as baptized people who belong to the Lord. This belonging translates itself as listening to God's word, participating in the offering, and communion in the Lord's love.

Today it is important to re-evangelize Sunday, for in many places its meaning has been obscured under pressure from an individualistic and materialistic culture. How can we rediscover the meaning of this

---

23. John Paul II, Apostolic Letter, *Dies Domini*, n. 19.

assembly of disciples around the risen Lord? By remembering our Christian roots, to which many eloquent voices testify. At the beginning of the fourth century in North Africa, some Christians preferred to die rather than live without Sunday, that is, without the Lord whom they encountered in the holy Eucharist. At the beginning of the third millennium these martyrs of Abitene give us pause to reflect and they intercede for us that we might rediscover the richness of the life-giving encounter with the risen Lord who gives himself in the Eucharist.

The world awaits this witness of the assembled Church, the sacrament of salvation by which it is secretly nourished.

PART THREE

For the Life of the World

The Church, the risen Lord's partner, lives because of this gift of God and, united to Jesus Christ, the High Priest, gives this gift to humanity. The world benefits from the love of Christians and the Church's worship that glorifies God by interceding for the world. Whether the Church dialogues with God in worship or in her mission to the world, the Church does not live for herself, but for the one who came "that they may have life, and have it abundantly" (*Jn* 10.10). The Church's life witnesses to the Lord's life shared in the holy Eucharist.

IV - The Eucharist, the Life of Christ in our Lives

A. The Spiritual Worship of the Baptized

One body in Jesus Christ

"Thus by baptism men are plunged into the paschal mystery of Christ: they die with Him, are buried with Him, and rise with Him; they receive the spirit of adoption as sons 'in which we cry: Abba,

Father' (*Rom* 8.15), and thus become true adorers whom the Father seeks (17)."[24] "... The water receives our body as a tomb, and so becomes the image of death while the Spirit pours in life-giving water, renewing in souls which were dead the life they first possessed."[25] Being baptized into the Church's faith introduces the faithful into the experience of the Paschal Mystery of Jesus Christ, who died to sin and lives for God. Going down into the water symbolizes death; coming up out of the water symbolizes the new life of the Christian who has committed him- or herself to following Jesus Christ in obedience to the Father through the Holy Spirit's power.

This is why Saint Paul urges the baptized to live a new life: "I appeal to you, therefore, brothers and sisters, by the mercies of God, to present your bodies as a living sacrifice, holy and acceptable to God, which is your spiritual worship." In the Pauline vision, this spiritual worship consists of our total self-offering in union with the whole Church.

It points to a totally renewed life: "So, whether you eat or drink, or whatever you do, do everything for

---

24. Second Vatican Council, Constitution on the Sacred Liturgy, *Sacrosanctum concilium*, n. 6.
25. Saint Basil the Great, *On the Holy Spirit*, translated by David Anderson. New York: St. Vladimir's Seminary Press, 1980. Chapter 15, § 35, p. 58-59.

the glory of God" (1 *Cor* 10.31). "Do not be conformed to this world, but be transformed by the renewing of your minds, so that you may discern what is the will of God" (*Rom* 12.2). This new worship shows itself, among other ways, by humility and service, "each according to the measure of faith that God has assigned" (*Rom* 12.3).

For, the Apostle continues, "as in one body we have many members, and not all the members have the same function, so we, who are many, are one body in Christ, and individually we are members one of another" (*Rom* 12.4-5). Spiritual worship consists of using our own gifts in a spirit of solidarity and humble service, with sincere love, in joy and, as far as possible, in peace with all. The Apostle concludes by recalling the constant struggle against the forces of evil in which Christians must engage: "Do not be overcome by evil, but overcome evil with good" (*Rom* 12.21). "The greatest sacrifice we can make to God," says Saint Cyprian, "is our peace, harmony among fellow Christians, a people united with the unity of the Father, the Son and the Holy Spirit."[26]

The life of Christ who nourishes our offering through the Eucharist, assimilates us to Him and

---

26. Saint Cyprian, *Treatise on the Lord's Prayer* (23-24: CSEL 3, 284-285), in *The Liturgy of the Hours*, Vol. III (New York: Catholic Book Publishing Corp., 1975), p. 377.

makes us available to others, in the unity of a single body and a single Spirit. Christ's life transforms the community into a temple of the living God for New Covenant worship. "If you are the body and members of Christ, then it is your sacrament that is placed on the table of the Lord; it is your sacrament that you receive. To that which you are you respond 'Amen' ('yes, it is true!') and by responding to it you assent to it. For you hear the words, 'the Body of Christ' and respond 'Amen.' Be then a member of the Body of Christ that your Amen may be true."[27] Here is the Christian sacrifice: That all are one body in Jesus Christ. The Church celebrates this mystery in the sacrament of the altar, where she learns to offer herself in the offering that she makes to God.

B. Authentic Adoration

The Father seeks adorers

The Eucharist makes Christ present in the act of adoration par excellence, his death on the Cross. By his act of absolute love unto death, Christ returns to the Father with reconciled humankind and obtains for all the Spirit of love and peace, the Spirit who gives life to the Church's adoration in spirit and in truth. Though Him, with Him and in Him, the whole Church adores in the name of redeemed humanity. In

---

27. Saint Augustine, *Sermo* 272: PL 38, 1247.

the offering of the holy Sacrifice *in persona Christi, Caput et Corpus,* as Saint Augustine puts it, including the active participation of the faithful in the mystery of praise, thanksgiving and communion, Christ and the Church carry out this supreme act of adoration.

This participation, which is, first of all, interior, is expressed in words and gestures: responses to the words of the presider, listening to the Word, songs, the Prayer of the Faithful, the Eucharistic acclamations – in particular the great Amen –, sharing the Bread of eternal life and the cup of salvation. All these actions express the royal priesthood of the baptized, which consecrates their primordial, inalienable dignity as human beings.

This act of adoration in which Christ and the Church engage in the Eucharistic Celebration does not end with the liturgy. It is prolonged in his permanent sacramental presence, which invites the faithful to participate by adoration of the Blessed Sacrament. Eucharistic adoration outside Mass prolongs the memorial by inviting the faithful to remain with the Lord who is present in the Blessed Sacrament: "The Teacher is here and is calling for you" (*Jn* 11.28). In Eucharistic adoration, the faithful recognize the Lord's real presence and join themselves to his act of self-offering to the Father. Their adoration shares in his adoration because it is through Him, with Him and in Him that all prayer and adoration are given to God and accepted by God. Is not Christ, who announced to the Samaritan woman that the Father was seeking those who adored in spirit and in truth (*Jn* 4.23-26), the first adorer who leads the long line of all men and women who adore? (*Heb* 12.2, 24).

"Living with Christ the Lord, they achieve a close familiarity with him and in his presence pour out their hearts for themselves and for those dear to them; they pray for peace and for the salvation of the world. Offering their entire lives with Christ to the Father in the Holy Spirit, they draw from this wondrous exchange an increase of faith, hope and love."[28] "It is pleasant to spend time with Him, to lie close to his breast like the Beloved Disciple (*cf. Jn* 13.25) and to feel the infinite love present in his heart. If in our time Christians must be distinguished above all by the 'art of prayer', how can we not feel a renewed need to spend time in spiritual converse, in silent adoration, in heartfelt love before Christ present in the Most Holy Sacrament?"[29]

Once again we are witnessing everywhere in the Church a fervent revival of this "art of prayer" that

---

28. *Holy Communion and Worship of the Eucharist Outside Mass*, n. 80.
29. John Paul II, Encyclical Letter, *Ecclesia de Eucharistia*, n. 25.

Pope John Paul II associated with Eucharistic adoration, which increases both the Church's witness to God's love and her intercession for the needs of the world. The practise of adoration reinforces in the faithful the sense of the sacredness of the Eucharistic Celebration which has, unfortunately, decreased in certain areas. Explicitly recognizing the divine presence in the sacred species outside of Mass contributes to promoting the faithful's active and interior participation in the celebration and helps them to see it as more than a social ritual.

The fruits of Eucharistic adoration also influence the spiritual worship we offer throughout the whole of life – doing God's will every day. Contemplating Christ in a state of self-offering and immolation in the Blessed Sacrament teaches us to give ourselves without limit, actively and passively, to the point of being given like the Eucharistic bread which is given from one hand to another in holy communion. Does not the One whom we visit and adore in the tabernacle teach us to persevere in love, day in and day out, welcoming the circumstances and events of life and everything about them, leaving out nothing but sin, as we try to produce as much fruit as possible? True adoration is the gift of self in love, the ecstasy of love in the present moment, for the glory of God and the service of the neighbour. In this way Christ's adoration, and the Church's, is sacramentally actualized in the celebration of the Eucharist, and is prolonged in the heart of the community and the faithful.

C. The Ministers of the New Covenant

Do this in memory of me

Fundamental to worship in the New Covenant is the active participation of the members of the people of God, whether they are lay faithful or ordained ministers. The presentation of offerings and the action of the minister symbolize in some ways the whole of this participation. "The bread and wine become in a sense a symbol of all that the Eucharistic assembly brings, on its own part, as an offering to God and offers spiritually."[30] By the mediation of the minister who acts in Christ's name and even in His Person *(in Persona Christi),* by pronouncing the words of consecration, Christ assumes the offering of the assembly into his own and transforms it into his Body and Blood.

"The apostles, in their recollections, which are called Gospels, handed down to us what Jesus commanded them to do. They tell us that he took bread, gave thanks and said: 'Do this in memory of me. This is my body.' In the same way he took the cup, he gave

---

30. John Paul II, Apostolic Letter, *Dominicae Cenae,* n. 9, February 19, 1980.

thanks and said: 'This is my blood.' The Lord gave this command to them alone. Ever since then we have constantly reminded one another of these things."[31]

The assembly that remembers becomes the sign of the Church. It is made up of members who are very different and yet who are bound to each other and to other communities in the universal Church. This Church of Christ, entrusted to Saint Peter and his successors, welcomes in the minister who acts in Christ's name in the heart of the assembly the sign that Christ presides at her celebration. The ministry of bishops and priests thus shows that this assembly always receives the Lord's memorial as a gift, a gift that the Church does not give to herself, but receives from the Father, "from whom every family in heaven and on earth takes its name" (*Eph* 3.14-15).

Such a responsibility calls the Lord's ministers, particularly in the Latin Church, to live the commitment to celibacy that configures the priest to Jesus Christ, Head and Spouse of the Church. "The Church, as the spouse of Jesus Christ, wishes to be loved by the priest in the total and exclusive manner in which Jesus Christ her head and spouse loved her.

---

31. Saint Justin, *Apology in Defense of the Christians I* (Apology I, 66-67: PG 6, 427-431), in *The Liturgy of the Hours*, Vol. II (New York: Catholic Book Publishing Corp., 1976), p. 694-695.

Priestly celibacy, then, is the gift of self in and with Christ to his Church and expresses the priest's service to the Church in and with the Lord."[32] Consequently celibacy remains, despite the lack of understanding on the part of the ambient culture, an unfathomable gift of God, as "a stimulus for pastoral charity,"[33] as a particular way of participating in the fatherhood of God and the fecundity of the Church. Profoundly rooted in the Eucharist, the joyful witness of a priest who is happy in his ministry is the first source of new vocations.

V - Eucharist and Mission

"The two disciples of Emmaus, upon recognizing the Lord, 'set out immediately' (*cf. Lk* 24.33), in order to report what they had seen and heard. Once we have truly met the Risen One, we cannot keep the Good News to ourselves and the joy we have experienced. The encounter with Christ, constantly intensified and deepened in the Eucharist, issues in the Church and in every Christian an urgent summons to testimony and evangelization."[34]

---

32. John Paul II, Apostolic Exhortation, *Pastores Dabo vobis,* 1992, n. 29.

33. Second Vatican Council, Decree on the Ministry and Life of Priests, *Presbyterorum Ordinis,* n. 16.

34. John Paul II, Apostolic Letter, *Mane nobiscum Domine,* n. 24.

A. Evangelization and the Transformation of the World

Source and summit of evangelization

"The joys and the hopes, the griefs and the anxieties of the men of this age, especially those who are poor or in any way afflicted, these are the joys and hopes, the griefs and anxieties of the followers of Christ."[35] When the Church celebrates the memorial of the death and resurrection of Christ, she never stops asking God "Remember, Lord," all those for whom Christ came to bring life. This constant prayer expresses the identity of the Church and its mission, for the Church knows that she is in solidarity with and responsible for the salvation of all humanity. Living from the Eucharist, the Church participates in Christ's universal prayer of intercession and brings to humanity the hope of eternal life.

The Church accomplishes her mission by evangelization that passes on faith in Christ and by the quest for justice and peace that transforms the world. However, the Eucharist is the source and the summit of evangelization and of the world's transformation. The Church has the power to awaken in those tempted by despair the hope of eternal life.

---

35. Second Vatican Council, Pastoral constitution on the Church in the Modern World, *Gaudium et Spes,* n. 1.

The Eucharist opens to sharing those who are tempted to close their hands. It highlights reconciliation instead of division. It puts life and human dignity at the centre of our faith commitment. In a society too often dominated by a "culture of death," which the search for individual comfort, money or power only intensifies, the Eucharist reminds us of the rights of the poor and the duty of justice and solidarity. It awakens the community to the immense gift of the New Covenant that calls all humanity to go beyond itself.

"For the Church, evangelizing means bringing the Good News into all the strata of humanity, and through its influence transforming humanity from within and making it new: 'Now I am making the whole of creation new.' But there is no new humanity if there are not first of all new persons renewed by Baptism and by lives lived according to the Gospel. The purpose of evangelization is therefore precisely this interior change, and if it had to be expressed in one sentence the best way of stating it would be to say that the Church evangelizes when she seeks to convert, solely through the divine power of the message she proclaims, both the personal and collective consciences of people, the activities in which they engage, and the lives and concrete milieu which are theirs." [36]

---

36. Paul VI, Apostolic Exhortation, *Evangelii nuntiandi*, n. 18.

From the Eucharistic centre of its life, the Church of Christ has often contributed to the construction of human communities, by reinforcing the bond of unity between persons and groups. Thus, Christian communities, even small and poor ones, have grown up among the people where they have set down roots. In some countries, Christ's Church has established the faith in new cultures, just as it did in America among the indigenous and European peoples.

In these areas, Christianity, through the efforts of believers, has never ceased to look for fresh solutions to the new problems that emerging human communities must confront. Christianity has often accompanied the birth, development and survival of peoples, as it did in the "New World," while the memorial of the Lord accompanied their religious and social development. Because of its strong social and spiritual value, Christianity helped build authentic community: the sharing of the Word and the Bread of life led Christians to share other human realities. God's gift took root in the life of the world.

In the American continent, as elsewhere, the Church started with a missionary vision. Its faith and ecclesiastical institutions gave birth to a local Church that, inspired by the first community in Jerusalem, helped shape the characteristics of this emerging people. This Church, like the society in which it took root, was marked by an initial dynamism: Ursulines and Hospitallers; Recollets and Jesuits, lay associates and secular priests crossed the ocean to proclaim the gospel of God in a new land.

In the mystical adventure of these men and women, which pushed them to the limits of physical endurance, courage and faith, the Church deeply identified with this growing country. By once again drawing on its roots in the Eucharist, the great missionary thrust that so marked the history of this country must continue and deepen as it faces the new challenges of secularization.

What have I done for my brother?

B. Constructing Peace through Justice and Charity

The Church witnesses among humanity to the gift given for the life of the world. Thus, the Eucharist is an ongoing challenge to the quality of life and love that the disciples of Christ experience. What have I done for my brother or sister? What have you done for me? "I was hungry, thirsty, a stranger, naked, sick, in prison" (see *Mt* 25.31-46). Is what we celebrate compatible with our social, familial, racial and ethnic relationships, with our political and economic life?

We consider the Paschal Mystery as the central event of human history; celebrating its memorial discloses our inconsistency each time we tolerate some form of misery, injustice, violence, exploitation, racism, or lack of freedom. The Eucharist summons Christians to participate in the ongoing restoration of the human condition and the world's plight; if we do not do this, then we are invited seriously to live the gospel call to conversion, "leave your gift there before the altar and go; first be reconciled to your brother or sister, and then come and offer your gift" (*Mt* 5.23-24).

The current world situation in particular summons the conscience of Christians in regard to the harrowing problem of respect for human life from conception to natural death, as well as that of the hunger and misery of masses of the world's peoples. Their plight invites Christians to a globalization of solidarity in the name of the inalienable dignity of the human person, above all when defenceless people are struck by natural catastrophes, laid low by the indiscriminate machinery of war and economic exploitation, and confined to refugee camps. All those whom misery has deprived of their condition as human beings are the neighbour for whom Christ has died. His "Eucharistic" heart has borne all the world's misery on the Cross and his Spirit urges us to take an option for the poor and for innocent victims, as he did – peacefully and effectively.

Following the example of John Paul II, Pope Benedict XVI has constantly appealed to human responsibility, particularly that of leaders and heads of state: "On the basis of available statistical data, it can be said that less than half of the immense sums spent worldwide on armaments would be more than sufficient to liberate the immense masses of the poor from destitution. This challenges humanity's conscience. To peoples living below the poverty line, more as a result of situations to do with international political, commercial and cultural relations than as a result of circumstances beyond anyone's control, our common commitment to truth can and must give new hope."[37]

"However, we know that evil does not have the last word, because it was the Crucified and Risen Christ who overcame it, and his triumph is expressed with the power of merciful love. His Resurrection gives us this certainty: despite all the darkness that exists in the world, evil does not have the last word. Sustained by this certainty, we will be able, with greater courage and enthusiasm, to commit ourselves to work for the birth of a more just world."[38]

---

37. Benedict XVI, Audience with the Diplomatic Corps accredited to the Holy See, January 9, 2006.
38. Benedict XVI, General audience, April 12, 2006.

VI - Witnesses to Eucharist in the Midst of the World

A. The Universal call to Holiness

Called to the perfection of love

God created man in his image and likeness (*Gen* 1.26): calling man into existence by love, God also calls him to love.[39] Vocations to love are as diverse as there are people. Baptismal grace shapes in them the love of Jesus Christ; the Eucharistic mystery nourishes and perfects it until it becomes a witness of holiness. No matter the state of life to which men and women have committed themselves – single, married or consecrated –, all are called to the perfection of love that Christ makes possible by the grace of redemption.

In the unity of the Christian life, different vocations are like rays of the one light of Christ "which shines out visibly from the Church." Lay people, because of the secular nature of their vocation, reflect the mystery of the Word Incarnate, the Alpha and Omega of the world, the foundation and measure of the value of all created realities. The sacred ministers are living images of Christ, leader and shepherd, who guides his people between the already and not yet, as they await his return in glory. Consecrated life

---

39. Second Vatican Council, Pastoral Constitution on the Church in the Modern World, *Gaudium et Spes*, n. 19.

should show the Son of God made man as the eschatological end point towards which everything is moving, the splendour before which all other light pales, the infinite beauty that alone can fill the human heart.

B. The Family, the Domestic Church, Foundation of a Civilization of Love

Christ's Body and Blood: the foundation of the family

"The Eucharist is the very source of Christian marriage. The Eucharistic Sacrifice, in fact, represents Christ's covenant of love with the Church, sealed with His Blood on the Cross. In this sacrifice of the New and Eternal Covenant, Christian spouses encounter the source from which their own marriage covenant flows, is interiorly structured and continuously renewed. As a representation of Christ's sacrifice of love for the Church, the Eucharist is a fountain of charity. In the Eucharistic gift of charity the Christian family finds the foundation and soul of its 'communion' and its 'mission': by partaking in the Eucharistic Bread, the different members of the Christian family become one body, which reveals and shares in the wider unity of the Church. Their sharing in the Body of Christ that is 'given up' and in His Blood that is 'shed' becomes a never-ending source of missionary and apostolic dynamism for the Christian family."[40]

The specific mission of the family is to enflesh love and put it at the service of society: conjugal love, paternal and maternal love, fraternal love, love of a community of persons and generations, love lived under the sign of a couple's faithfulness and fecundity for a civilization of life and love. So that this witness concretely touches the life of society, the Church calls families to be assiduous in attending Sunday Mass. For by drinking at the source of this love, the family will protect its own stability. Moreover, by thus strengthening its consciousness of being the domestic Church, the family participates more actively in witnessing to the faith and love that the Church incarnates in the heart of society.

Today the witness of the domestic Church is marked by the sign of the cross, for example, when one spouse is unfaithful to their commitment or when one or more children no longer practise the faith and Christian values that their parents tried to give them, or when families are divided and blended after a divorce and remarriage. In these painful experiences, does not Christ call abandoned spouses, hurting children and broken-hearted parents to

---

40. John Paul II, Apostolic Exhortation, *Familiaris Consortio*, n. 37.

share in a special way in his own experience of death and Resurrection? The difficult and complex situations of today's families invite pastors to a profound pastoral charity so that they can welcome all families and encourage all who live in irregular situations to participate in the Eucharist and community life, even when they cannot receive Holy Communion.

Consecrated life: my vocation is love

C. Consecrated life, Pledge of hope that Proclaims the Bridegroom's Coming

"By its very nature the Eucharist is at the centre of the consecrated life, both for individuals and for communities. It is the daily viaticum and source of the spiritual life for the individual and for the Institute. By means of the Eucharist all consecrated persons are called to live Christ's Paschal Mystery, uniting themselves to Him by offering their own lives to the Father through the Holy Spirit. Frequent and prolonged adoration of Christ present in the Eucharist enables us in some way to relive Peter's experience at the Transfiguration: 'It is well that we are here'. In the celebration of the mystery of the Lord's Body and Blood, the unity and charity of those who have consecrated their lives to God are strengthened and increased." [41]

---

41. John Paul II, Apostolic Exhortation, *Vita Consecrata*, n. 95.

"'What would become of the world if there were no religious'? Beyond all superficial assessments of its usefulness, consecrated life is important precisely in its being unbounded generosity and love, and this all the more so in a world which risks being suffocated in the whirlpool of the ephemeral. 'Without this concrete sign there would be a danger that the charity which animates the entire Church would grow cold, that the salvific paradox of the Gospel would be blunted, and that the 'salt' of faith would lose its savour in a world undergoing secularization'. The Church and society itself need people capable of devoting themselves totally to God and to others for the love of God." [42]

"If I speak in the tongues of mortals and of angels, but do not have love, I am nothing ... Love never ends. ... And now faith, hope, and love abide, these three; and the greatest of these is love" (1 *Cor* 13.1,8,13). Theresa of the Child Jesus, in her Carmelite monastery, discovered her vocation as she read the words of the apostle on the outstanding nature of love: "My vocation is love," she wrote. "In the heart of the Church, my Mother, I shall be love. Thus shall I be everything, and thus my dream will be realized."

---

42. *Ibid.*, n. 105.

Overcome by the merciful love of God the Father, she took advantage of every moment of her life to embrace Jesus, her All, and to witness to this relationship by contemplation and service. Praying for criminals, walking for missionaries, supporting priests by acts of penance, forming novices in the perfection of love, Therese is recognized as the modern icon of consecrated life: master of the little way, universal patron of missions, doctor of the Church. "I do not regret having surrendered myself to love," she said, shortly before her death.

The Synod on the Eucharist of October 2005 spoke in this way of consecrated persons: "Your Eucharistic witness in the service of Christ is a cry of love in the darkness of the world, an echo of the ancient Marian hymns, the *Stabat Mater* and the *Magnificat*. May the Woman of the Eucharist par excellence, crowned with stars, and rich in love, the Virgin of the Assumption and of the Immaculate Conception, watch over you in your service of God and the poor, in the joy of Easter, for the hope of the world."[43]

---

43. Synod on the Eucharist, *Message to the People of God,* n. 20, 21, October 2005.

CONCLUSION

God so loved the World

By way of conclusion, a few texts of Vatican II will synthesize the Trinitarian, nuptial and missionary perspectives that we wish to give to the theme of the International Eucharistic Congress of 2008. God so loved the world that he gave his only Son so that through Him, with Him and in Him, the world might live the Trinitarian life. The Holy Eucharist is God's gift par excellence, a wedding present, welcomed and celebrated by the Church, which makes the Church the universal sacrament of the New Covenant. This gift of love essentially commits the Church to the Holy Spirit's mission, as it encounters humanity's universal desire for freedom in love.

"For God's Word, through Whom all things were made, was Himself made flesh and dwelt on the earth of men (see *Jn* 1.3,14). Thus, He entered the world's history as a perfect man, taking that history up into Himself and summarizing it (*Eph* 1.10). He Himself revealed to us that 'God is love' (1 *Jn* 4:8) and at the same time taught us that the new command of love was the basic law of human perfection and hence of the world's transformation."[44]

"When the work which the Father gave the Son to do on earth (see *Jn* 17.4) was accomplished, the Holy Spirit was sent on the day of Pentecost in order that He might continually sanctify the Church, and thus, all those who believe would have access through Christ in one Spirit to the Father (*cf. Eph* 2.18). He is the Spirit of Life, a fountain of water springing up to life eternal (*cf. Jn* 4.14; 7.38-39). ... The Spirit dwells in the Church ... By the power of the Gospel He makes the Church keep the freshness of youth. Uninterruptedly He renews it and leads it to perfect union with its Spouse (see *Rev* 22.17). The Spirit and the Bride both say to Jesus, the Lord, 'Come!' (17). Thus, the Church has been seen as 'a people made one with the unity of the Father, the Son and the Holy Spirit.'"[45]

"While helping the world and receiving many benefits from it, the Church has a single intention: that God's kingdom may come, and that the salvation of the whole human race may come to pass. For every benefit which the People of God during its earthly pilgrimage can offer to the human family stems from

---

44. Second Vatican Council, Pastoral Constitution on the Church in the Modern World, *Gaudium et Spes*, n. 38.

45. Second Vatican Council, Dogmatic Constitution, *Lumen Gentium*, n. 4

the fact that the Church is 'the universal sacrament of salvation', simultaneously manifesting and arising from the mystery of God's love." [46]

"The Lord left behind a pledge of this hope and strength for life's journey in that sacrament of faith where natural elements refined by man are changed into His glorified Body and Blood, providing a meal of brotherly solidarity and a foretaste of the heavenly banquet." [47]

"The Most Blessed Eucharist contains the entire spiritual boon of the Church, that is, Christ himself, our Pasch and Living Bread, by the action of the Holy Spirit through his very flesh vital and vitalizing, giving life to men who are thus invited and encouraged to offer themselves, their labors and all created things, together with Him." [48]

---

46. Second Vatican Council, Pastoral Constitution on the Church in the Modern World, *Gaudium et Spes*, n. 45.

47. *Ibid.*, n. 38.

48. Second Vatican Council, Decree on the Ministry and Life of Priests, *Presbyterorum Ordinis*, n. 5.

CONCLUSION

Bread yourself, good Shepherd, tend us;
Jesus, with your love befriend us.
You refresh us and defend us;
to your lasting goodness send us
That the land of life we see.
Lord, who all things both rule and know,
who on this earth such food bestow,
Grant that we your saints may follow
to the banquet you make hallow,
With them heirs and guests to be. [49]

---

49. Saint Thomas Aquinas, Eucharistic hymn, *Lauda Sion*.

MEMBER OF SCABRINI GROUP
Québec, Canada
2007